Meet the SEA LION

Susanna Keller

PowerKiDS press
New York

Published in 2010 by The Rosen Publishing Group, Inc.
29 East 21st Street, New York, NY 10010

First Edition

Editor: Amelie von Zumbusch
Book Design: Kate Laczynski
Photo Researcher: Jessica Gerweck

Photo Credits: Cover, pp. 1, 4, 12, 18, 20, 22, 24 (pup, trick) Shutterstock.com; p. 6 © www.agefotostock.com/Rudi von Briel; pp. 8, 24 (flipper) © www.istockphoto.com/Laurel Stewart; pp. 10, 24 (whiskers) © www.istockphoto.com/Lloyd Luecke; p. 14 © www.istockphoto.com/Krzysztof Wiktor; p. 16 Getty Images/Andy Rouse.

Library of Congress Cataloging-in-Publication Data

Keller, Susanna.
  Meet the sea lion / Susanna Keller. — 1st ed.
      p. cm. — (At the zoo)
  Includes index.
  ISBN 978-1-4358-9308-5 (library binding) — ISBN 978-1-4358-9728-1 (pbk.) — ISBN 978-1-4358-9729-8 (6 pack)
  1. Sea lions—Juvenile literature. I. Title.
  QL737.P63K45 2010
  599.79'75—dc22
                                   2009017845

Manufactured in the United States of America

CPSIA Compliance Information: Batch #WW10PK: For Further Information contact Rosen Publishing, New York, New York at 1-800-237-9932

CONTENTS

These animals are sea lions. Sea lions live much of their lives in the water.

Sea lions live in the Pacific Ocean and the Indian Ocean. You can also see sea lions in zoos.

Sea lions have short brown fur. They also have a tail and two **flippers**.

Sea lions have ears that stick out from their heads. Sea lions have **whiskers**, too.

Baby sea lions are **pups**. Pups are born on land. They learn to swim when they are a few weeks old.

Fish are a sea lion's main food. Sea lions also eat other small sea animals, such as crabs.

16

Sea lions are good swimmers. They can stay underwater for as long as 40 minutes.

18

A sea lion can be very loud! It barks, roars, and honks.

Sea lions are very playful. This makes them lots of fun to watch.

Sea lions are smart. They can learn to do **tricks**, such as walking on their flippers.

WORDS TO KNOW

flipper

pup

trick

whiskers

WEB SITES

Due to the changing nature of Internet links, PowerKids Press has developed an online list of Web sites related to the subject of this book. This site is updated regularly. Please use this link to access the list:
www.powerkidslinks.com/atzoo/sealion/